mance

...chs. All rights reserved.
...y be used or reproduced
...rmission except in the
...or information, write
...Meel Universal company,
...souri 64111.

... 5 4 3 2 1

...: 2003102690

...inesses

...ity discounts with bulk
...romotional use. For
...epartment, Andrews
...City, Missouri 64111.

The Cats' Book of A...

Copyright © 2003 by Kate Ledger and Lisa S...
Printed in Singapore. No part of this book m...
in any manner whatsoever without written ...
case of reprints in the context of reviews. ...
Andrews McMeel Publishing, an Andrews Mc...
4520 Main Street, Kansas City, Mi...

03 04 05 06 07 TWP 10 9 8 7

ISBN: 0-7404-3846-

Library of Congress Control Numb...

Attention: Schools and Bu...

Andrews McMeel books are available at quar...
purchase for educational, business, or sales
information, please write to: Special Sales
McMeel Publishing, 4520 Main Street, Kans...

For Ben and Jonny

*H*ome is in
each other's arms.

*L*earn to be
a supportive listener.

*T*reasure mementos
from when you first met.

Look after one another.

If you're the first
to wake, bring breakfast
in bed.

*T*ake interest in
each other's hobbies.

*R*emember your anniversary.

Plan a romantic evening at home.

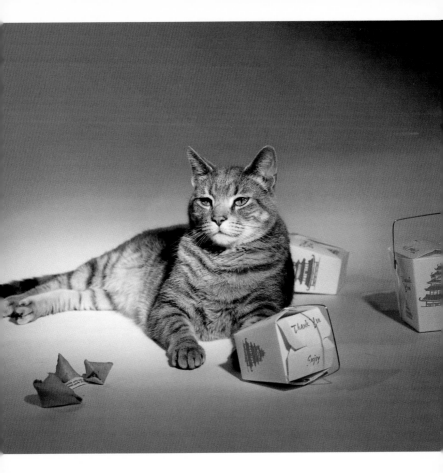

Fall asleep together under the stars.

Share.

Sometimes nobody
wants to do the laundry.

*N*ever go to bed angry.

*A*sk directions.

*W*atch the sunset together.

Honesty is the
best policy.

*A*dmit when
you're wrong.

*Whisper
sweet nothings.*

*Everyone needs
time alone.*

*T*reat each other
like royalty.

Memorize
each other's features.

Don't stay away
too long.

*M*ake up tenderly
after an argument.

*M*aintain friendships
outside your relationship.

It takes a positive
self-image to be a
good partner.

*P*lan to grow old
side by side.

*M*ake time to
dine together.

$\mathcal{T}$he most
intimate moments
require no words.

Live happily ever after.